The Glorious Christmas
SONGBOOK

A CLASSIC ILLUSTRATED EDITION

In memory of Gene Autry

—C.E. and B.D.

Book design by Susan Van Horn.
Typeset in Pabst Oldstyle and Mrs. Eaves.
Music notation by Robert Puff, RPM, Seattle, Washington.
Printed in Hong Kong.
ISBN 0-8118-2204-4

Library of Congress Cataloging-in-Publication Data available.

Distributed in Canada by Raincoast Books
8680 Cambie Street, Vancouver, British Columbia V6P 6M9

10 9 8 7 6 5 4 3 2 1

Chronicle Books
85 Second Street, San Francisco, California 94105

www.chroniclebooks.com/Kids

The Glorious Christmas SONGBOOK

A CLASSIC ILLUSTRATED EDITION

Compiled by Cooper Edens

and Benjamin Darling

chronicle books · san francisco

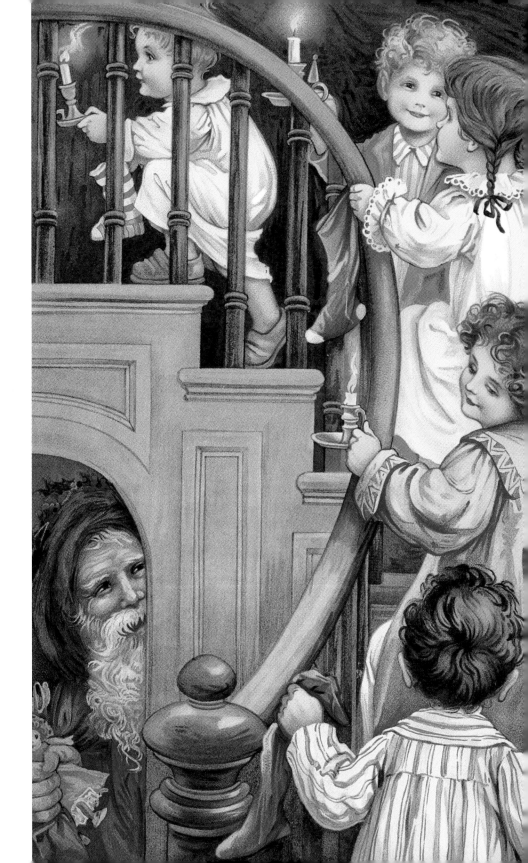

PREFACE

From generation to generation, Christmas songs have been handed down like sparkling tree ornaments — each one special, meaningful, and familiar. Every year, these songs reappear, and we find ourselves singing, whistling, and humming them. From *All I Want for Christmas Is My Two Front Teeth* to *Silent Night* to *Winter Wonderland*, the songs that define the season have been sung for so long they are part of our collective songbook.

In *The Glorious Christmas Songbook* you will find the old and the new; the joyous and the jolly; the spiritual and the sentimental — those songs that have been and will be sung for many Christmases to come.

It gave us great joy to pair these memorable songs with illustrations from antique picture books, postcards, and magazine covers. For us, the book fell into place easily as if these favorite lyrics and fond images were being reunited after existing together once before at some wondrous time. The result, we hope, is a treasury that will sing its way into the hearts and memories of all who celebrate the holidays.

—*Cooper Edens & Benjamin Darling*

Contents

It's Beginning to Look Like Christmas

[WILLSON]

It's beginning to look a lot like Chrismas, everywhere you go.
Take a look at the five and ten, glistening once again
With candy canes and silver lanes aglow.

It's beginning to look a lot like Christmas, toys in ev'ry store.
But the prettiest sight you'll see, is the holly that will be
On your own front door.

A pair of Hop-a-long boots and a pistol that shoots
Is the wish of Barney and Ben.
Dolls that will talk and go for a walk
Is the hope of Janice and Jen.
And Mom and Dad can hardly wait for school to start again.

It's beginning to look a lot like Christmas, everywhere you go.
There's a tree in the grand hotel, one in the park as well,
The sturdy kind that doesn't mind the snow.

It's beginning to look a lot like Christmas, soon the bells will start.
And the thing that will make them ring, is the carol that you sing
Right within your heart.

It's be - gin - ning to look a lot like Christ - mas,____ ev - ery - where you go. Take a look at the five and ten, glis - ten - ing once a-gain With can - dy canes and sil - ver lanes a - glow.

Let It Snow! Let It Snow! Let It Snow!

[CAHN AND STYNE]

Oh the weather outside is frightful
But the fire is so delightful,
And since we've no place to go,
Let it snow! Let it snow! Let it snow!

It doesn't show signs of stopping
And I brought some corn for popping,
The lights are turned way down low,
Let it snow! Let it snow! Let it snow!

When we finally kiss goodnight
How I'll hate going out in the storm!
But if you'll really hold me tight
All the way home I'll be warm.

The fire is slowly dying
And my dear, we're still good-bying,
But as long as you love me so,
Let it snow! Let it snow! Let it snow!

Santa Claus Is Coming to Town

[GILLESPIE AND COOTS]

You better watch out,
You better not cry,
Better not pout,
I'm telling you why:
Santa Claus is comin' to town.

He's making a list
And checking it twice,
Gonna find out
Who's naughty and nice:
Santa Claus is comin' to town.

He sees you when you're sleeping,
He knows when you're awake.
He knows if you've been bad or good,
So be good for goodness sake.

Oh! you better watch out,
You better not cry,
Better not pout,
I'm telling you why:
Santa Claus is comin' to town.

You bet-ter watch out, You bet-ter not cry,

Bet-ter not pout, I'm tel-ling you why:

Winter Wonderland

[Bernard and Smith]

Sleigh bells ring, are you list'nin?
In the lane, snow is glist'nin,
A beautiful sight, we're happy tonight,
Walkin' in a winter wonderland!

Gone away is the bluebird,
Here to stay is a new bird,
He sings a love song, as we go along,
Walkin' in a winter wonderland!

In the meadow we can build a snowman,
Then pretend that he is Parson Brown;
He'll say, "Are you married?" We'll say, "No man!
But you can do the job when you're in town!"

Later on we'll conspire
As we dream by the fire,
To face unafraid, the plans that we made,
Walkin' in a winter wonderland!

14

The Holly and the Ivy

[TRADITIONAL ENGLISH CAROL]

The holly and the ivy,
When they are both full grown,
Of all the trees that are in the wood,
The holly bears the crown.

The rising of the sun,
And running of the deer,
The playing of the merry organ,
Sweet singing in the choir.

The hol-ly and the i - vy, When

they are both full grown, Of— all the trees that are

in the wood, The— hol-ly bears the crown.

Deck the Hall

[Welsh Traditional Carol]

Deck the hall with boughs of holly,

Fa la la la la, la la la la.

'Tis the season to be jolly,

Fa la la la la, la la la la.

Don we now our gay apparel,

Fa la la, la la la, la la la.

Troll the ancient yuletide carol.

Fa la la la la, la la la la.

See the blazing yule before us,

Fa la la la la, la la la la.

Strike the harp and join the chorus,

Fa la la la la, la la la la.

Follow me in merry measure,

Fa la la, la la la, la la la.

While I tell of yuletide treasure.

Fa la la la la, la la la la.

Fast away the old year passes,

Fa la la la la, la la la la.

Hail the new, ye lads and lasses,

Fa la la la la, la la la la.

Sing we joyous, all together,

Fa la la, la la la, la la la.

Heedless of the wind and weather.

Fa la la la la, la la la la.

Deck the hall with boughs of hol-ly, Fa la la la la, la la la la.

'Tis the sea-son to be jol-ly, Fa la la la la, la la la la.

Infant Holy, Infant Lowly

[POLISH CAROL]

Infant holy, Infant lowly,
For his bed a cattle-stall;
Oxen lowing, little knowing
Christ the babe is Lord of all.
Swiftly winging angels singing,
Noëls ringing, tidings bringing:
Christ the babe is Lord of all.

Flocks were sleeping, shepherds keeping
Vigil till the morning new;
Saw the glory, heard the story,
Tidings of gospel true.
Thus rejoicing, free from sorrow,
Praises voicing, greet the morrow:
Christ the babe was born for you.

In - fant ho - ly,   In - fant low - ly,

For his bed   a   cat - tle - stall;

It Came upon a Midnight Clear

[SEARS AND WILLIS]

It came upon a midnight clear,
That glorious song of old,
From angels bending near the earth
To touch their harps of gold.

Peace on the earth, good will to men
From heaven's all gracious King.
The world in solemn stillness
Lay to hear the angels sing.

Still through the cloven skies they come,
With peaceful wings unfurl'd;
And still their heav'nly music floats
O'er all the weary world.

Above its sad and lowly plains
They bend on hov'ring wing.
And ever o'er its Babel sounds
The blessed angels sing.

It came up - on —— a mid - night clear, That glo - rious song —— of old

19

Toyland

[MacDonough and Herbert]

Toyland! Toyland!
Little girl and boy land,
While you dwell within it
You are ever happy then.

Childhood's joyland,
Mystic, merry joyland,
Once you pass its borders
You can never return again.

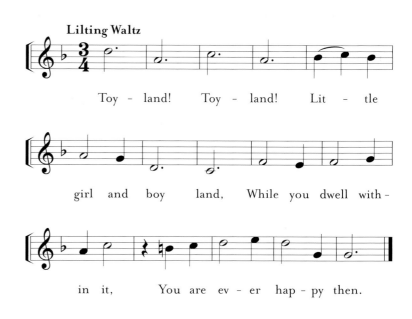

Lilting Waltz

Toy - land! Toy - land! Lit - tle
girl and boy land, While you dwell with -
in it, You are ev - er hap - py then.

Rudolph, the Red-nosed Reindeer

[Marks]

Ru-dolph the red - nosed rein - deer

Had a ver-y shin-y nose, and if you ev - er

saw it, You would e-ven say it glows.

You know Dasher and Dancer and Prancer and Vixen,
Comet and Cupid and Donner and Blitzen,
But do you recall the most famous reindeer of all?

Rudolph, the red-nosed reindeer
Had a very shiny nose,
And if you ever saw it,
You would even say it glows.

All of the other reindeer
Used to laugh and call him names,
They never let poor Rudolph,
Join in any reindeer games.

Then one foggy Christmas Eve,
Santa came to say,
"Rudolph with your nose so bright,
Won't you guide my sleigh tonight?"

Then how the reindeer loved him
As they shouted out with glee:
"Rudolph, the red-nosed reindeer,
You'll go down in history!"

It's the Most Wonderful Time of the Year

[POLA AND WYLE]

It's the most wonderful time of the year,
With the kid's jingle belling
And everyone telling
You be of good cheer;
It's the most wonderful time of the year.

It's the hap… happiest season of all,
With those holiday greetings
And gay happy meetings
When friends come to call.
It's the most hap… happiest season of all.

There'll be parties for hosting,
Marshmallows for toasting
And caroling out in the snow.
There'll be scary ghost stories
And tales of the glories
Of Christmases long long ago.

It's the most wonderful time of the year.
There'll be much mistletoeing
And hearts will be glowing
When loved ones are near.
It's the most wonderful time of the year.

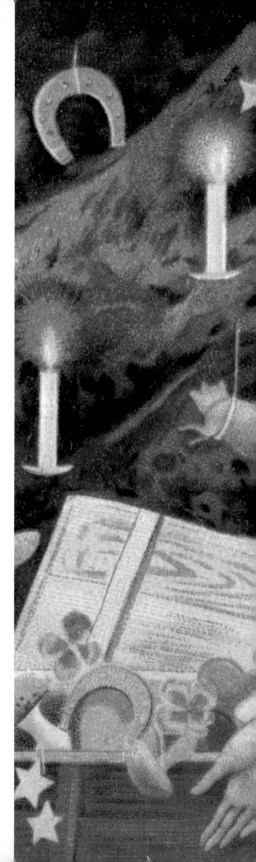

The Twelve Days of Christmas

[TRADITIONAL ENGLISH ROUND]

On the twelfth day of Christmas

My true love gave to me

Twelve drummer's drumming,

Eleven pipers piping,

Ten lords a-leaping,

Nine ladies dancing,

Eight maids a-milking,

Seven swans a-swimming,

Six geese a-laying,

Five golden rings,

Four calling birds,

Three French hens,

Two turtle doves,

And a partridge in a pear tree.

On the first day of Christ-mas My true love gave to me   A par-tridge— in a pear   tree.——

O Holy Night

[ADAM AND CAPPEAU]

O Holy Night!
The stars are brightly shining.
It is the night of the dear Savior's birth.
Long lay the world in sin and error pining
Till he appeared and the soul felt its worth.

A thrill of hope the weary world rejoices,
For yonder breaks a new and glorious morn,
Fall on your knees! O hear the angels' voices!

O night divine! O night when Christ was born,
O night divine! O night, O night divine!

Flowing

O   Ho-ly   Night!— The stars are brightly shin -

ing, It is the night of our dear Sav-ior's birth.

Hark! The Herald Angels Sing

[Wesley and Mendelssohn]

Hark! The Herald Angels Sing,
"Glory to the new-born King!
Peace on earth, and mercy mild,
God and sinners reconciled."

Joyful, all ye nations rise,
Join the triumph of the skies;
With th' angelic host proclaim,
"Christ is born in Bethlehem."

Hark! The Her - ald An - gels Sing,—

"Glo-ry to the new-born King! Peace on earth, and

mer-cy mild,_ God and sin - ners re-con-ciled."

The Christmas Song

[TORMÉ AND WELLS]

Chestnuts roasting on an open fire,
Jack Frost nipping at your nose,
Yuletide carols being sung by a choir
And folks dressed up like Eskimos.

Ev'rybody knows a turkey and some mistletoe
Help to make the season bright.
Tiny tots with their eyes all a-glow
Will find it hard to sleep tonight.

They know that Santa's on his way,
He's loaded lots of toys and goodies on his sleigh
And ev'ry mother's child is gonna spy
To see if reindeer really know how to fly.

And so I'm offering this simple phrase
To kids from one to ninety two.
Altho' it's been said many times, many ways
"Merry Christmas to you."

Moderately

Chest - nuts roast-ing on an o - pen fire, Jack Frost nip-ping at your nose

Here Comes Santa Claus

[AUTRY AND HALDMAN]

Here comes Santa Claus! Here comes Santa Claus!
Right down Santa Claus Lane!
Vixen and Blitzen and all his reindeer pulling on the rein.
Bells are ringing, children singing, all is merry and bright.
Hang your stockings and say your pray'rs
'Cause Santa Claus comes tonight.

Here comes Santa Claus! Here comes Santa Claus!
Right down Santa Claus Lane!
He's got a bag that is filled with toys for the boys and girls again.
Hear those sleighbells jingle jangle, what a beautiful sight.
Jump in bed, cover up your head,
'Cause Santa Claus comes tonight.

Here comes Santa Claus! Here comes Santa Claus!
Right down Santa Claus Lane!
He doesn't care if you're rich or poor for he loves you just the same.
Santa knows that we're God's children, that makes ev'rything right.
Fill your hearts with a Christmas cheer,
'Cause Santa Claus comes tonight.

Here comes San - ta Claus! Here comes San - ta Claus! Right down San - ta Claus Lane!

All I Want for Christmas Is My Two Front Teeth

[GARDNER]

Ev'rybody stops and stares at me
These two teeth are gone as you can see
I don't know just who to blame for this catastrophe!
But my one wish on Christmas Eve is plain as it can be!

All I want for Christmas is my two front teeth,
My two front teeth, see my two front teeth!
Gee, if I could only have my two front teeth,
Then I could wish you, "Merry Christmas!"

It seems so long since I could say,
"Sister Susie sitting on a thistle!"
Gosh oh gee, how happy I'd be,
If I could only whistle (thhh.)

All I want for Christmas is my two front teeth,
My two front teeth, see my two front teeth.
Gee, if I could only have my two front teeth,
Then I could wish you, "Merry Christmas!"

Brightly

All I want for Christ-mas is my two front teeth, My two front teeth, see my two front teeth!

I Am Christmas

[TRADITIONAL GERMAN ICE DANCE]

Now dance I say,
Now dance I say!
I am Christmas,
And I dance away!
We dance and skate away.

Now have good day,
Now have good day!
I am Christmas,
And I sing my way!
We sing and go my way.

Energetically

Now dance I say, Now dance I

say! I am Christ - mas, And I

dance a - way!_____ We dance and

skate a - way._____

Angels We Have Heard On High

[FRENCH TRADITIONAL]

Angels we have heard on high
Sweetly singing o'er the plains,
And the mountains in reply,
Echoing their joyous strains.

Gloria in excelsis Deo,
Gloria in excelsis Deo.

Shepherds, why this jubilee?
Why your joyous strains prolong?
What the gladsome tidings be
Which inspire your heavenly song?

Gloria in excelsis Deo,
Gloria in excelsis Deo.

Come to Bethlehem and see
Him whose birth the angels sing.
Come, adore on bended knee
Christ the Lord, the new-born King!

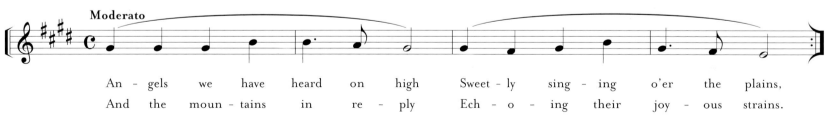

An - gels we have heard on high Sweet-ly sing - ing o'er the plains,
And the moun - tains in re - ply Ech - o - ing their joy - ous strains.

O Come, All Ye Faithful

[WADE AND OAKELEY]

O come, all ye faithful,
Joyful and triumphant,
O come ye, O come ye, to Bethlehem.
Come and behold Him, born the King of angels.
O come, let us adore Him,
O come, let us adore Him,
O come, let us adore Him,
Christ, the Lord.

Sing, choirs of angels,
Sing in exultation;
Sing all ye citizens of heav'n above:
Glory to God in the highest.
O come, let us adore Him,
O come, let us adore Him,
O come, let us adore Him,
Christ, the Lord.

Yea, Lord, we greet Thee,
Born this happy morning;
Jesus, to Thee be glory giv'n;
Word of the Father, now in flesh appearing.
O come, let us adore Him,
O come, let us adore Him,
O come, let us adore Him,
Christ, the Lord.

O come, all ye faith-ful, Joy-ful and tri-um-phant, O

come ye, O come ye, to Beth - le - hem.

I'll Be Home for Christmas

[GANNON AND KENT]

I'll be home for Christmas,
You can count on me.
Please have snow and mistletoe
And presents on the tree.

Christmas Eve will find me
Where the love light gleams.
I'll be home for Christmas,
If only in my dreams.

Moderately

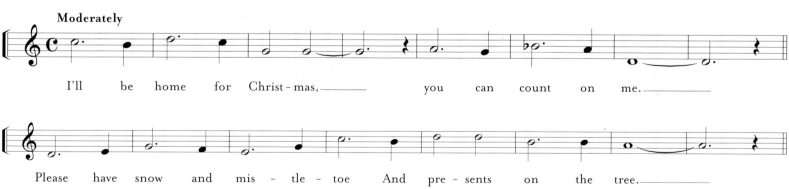

I'll be home for Christ-mas,_____ you can count on me._____

Please have snow and mis - tle - toe And pre - sents on the tree._____

The Wassail Song

[TRADITIONAL ENGLISH CAROL]

Here we come a-wassailing
Among the leaves so green;
Here we come a-wand'ring,
So fair to be seen:

Love and joy come to you,
And to you your wassail too;
And God bless you, and send you
A Happy New Year,
And God send you a Happy New Year.

God bless the Master of this house,
Likewise the Mistress too,
And all the little children
That round the table go.

Love and joy come to you,
And to you your wassail too;
And God bless you, and send you
A Happy New Year,
And God send you a Happy New Year.

And God bless you, and send— you A Hap - py New Year, and God send you a Hap - py New Year.

We Wish You A Merry Christmas

[TRADITIONAL ENGLISH CAROL]

We wish you a Merry Christmas,
We wish you a Merry Christmas,
We wish you a Merry Christmas
And a happy New Year.

Good tidings we bring
To you and your kin,
Good tidings for Christmas
And a happy New Year.

Now bring us some figgy pudding,
Now bring us some figgy pudding,
Now bring us some figgy pudding,
And bring it out here.

O we won't go until we've got some,
We won't go until we've got some,
We won't go until we've got some,
So bring it out here.

O we all like figgy pudding,
Yes, we all like figgy pudding,
We all like figgy pudding,
So bring it out here.

We wish you a mer-ry Christmas, and a

hap - py New Year.

Rockin' Around the Christmas Tree

[MARKS]

Rockin' around the Christmas Tree
At the Christmas party hop.
Mistletoe hung where you can see
Ev'ry couple tries to stop.

Rockin' around the Christmas Tree
Let the Christmas spirit ring.
Later we'll have some pumpkin pie
And we'll do some caroling.

You will get a sentimental feeling
When you hear voices singing,
"Let's be jolly.
Deck the halls with boughs of holly."

Rockin' around the Christmas Tree
Have a happy holiday.
Ev'ryone dancing merrily
In the new old fashioned way.

We Three Kings of Orient Are

[HOPKINS]

We three kings of Orient are,
Bearing gifts we traverse afar,
Field and fountain,
Moor and mountain,
Following yonder star.

O, Star of wonder,
Star of night,
Star with royal beauty bright,
Westward leading,
Still proceeding,
Guide us to Thy perfect light.

Born a King on Bethlehem's plain,
Gold I bring to crown Him again,
King forever,
Ceasing never,
Over us all to reign.

Good King Wenceslas

[Neale]

Good King Wenceslas looked out on the Feast of Stephen,
When the snow lay 'round about, deep and crisp and even.
Brightly shone the moon that night, though the frost was cruel.
When a poor man came in sight, gath'ring winter fuel.

"Hither page, and stand by me, if thou know'st it, telling,
Yonder peasant, who is he? Where and what his dwelling?"
"Sire, he lives a good league hence, underneath the mountain;
Right against the forest fence, by Saint Agnes' fountain."

"Bring me flesh and bring me wine, bring me pine-logs hither;
Thou and I will see him dine, when we bear them thither."
Page and monarch forth they went, forth they went together;
Through the rude wind's wild lament, and the bitter weather.

"Sire, the night is darker now, and the wind blows stronger;
Fails my heart, I know not how, I can go no longer."
"Mark my footsteps, my good page! Tread thou in them boldly:
Thou shalt find the winter's rage, freeze thy blood less coldly."

In his master's steps he trod, where the snow lay dinted;
Heat was in the very sod, which the saint had printed.
Therefore, Christian men, be sure, wealth or rank possessing,
Ye who now will bless the poor, shall yourself find blessing.

Good King Wen - ces - las looked out
When the snow lay 'round a - bout,

on the Feast of Ste - phen,
deep and crisp and e - ven.

I Saw Three Ships

[ENGLISH TRADITIONAL]

I saw three ships come sailing in,
On Christmas Day, on Christmas Day.
I saw three ships come sailing in,
On Christmas Day in the morning.

And what was in those ships all three,
On Christmas Day, on Christmas Day?
And what was in those ships all three,
On Christmas Day in the morning?

The Virgin Mary and Christ were there,
On Christmas Day, on Christmas Day.
The Virgin Mary and Christ were there,
On Christmas Day in the morning.

O Christmas Tree

[TRADITIONAL GERMAN CAROL]

O Christmas tree,
O Christmas tree,
You stand in verdant beauty!
O Christmas tree,
O Christmas tree,
You stand in verdant beauty!

Your boughs are green in summer's glow.
And do not fade in winter's snow.

O Christmas tree,
O Christmas tree,
You stand in verdant beauty!

O Christ-mas tree, O Christ-mas tree, You stand in ver-dant beau-ty! O beau-ty! Your

boughs are green in sum-mer's glow. And do not fade in win-ter's snow. O beau-ty!

Go Tell It on the Mountain

[Traditional American Spiritual]

While shepherds kept their watching
O'er silent flocks by night,
Behold throughout the heavens
There shone a holy light.

Go tell it on the mountain
Over the hills and everywhere,
Go tell it on the mountain
That Jesus Christ was born.

The shepherds feared and trembled
When lo! above the earth
Rang out the angel chorus
That hailed our Savior's birth.

Go tell it on the mountain
Over the hills and everywhere,
Go tell it on the mountain
That Jesus Christ was born.

Go tell it on the moun - tain   O - ver the hills and ever - y - where

Up on the Housetop

[Hanby]

Up on the housetop reindeer pause,
Out jumps good old Santa Claus;
Down thro' the chimney with lots of toys,
All for the little ones, Christmas joys.

Ho, ho, ho! Who wouldn't go?
Ho, ho, ho! Who wouldn't go?
Up on the housetop, click, click, click,
Down thro' the chimney...with good Saint Nick.

First comes the stocking of little Nell,
Oh, dear Santa, fill it well;
Give her a dollie that laughs and cries,
One that will open and shut her eyes.

Ho, ho, ho! Who wouldn't go?
Ho, ho, ho! Who wouldn't go?
Up on the housetop, click, click, click,
Down thro' the chimney...with good Saint Nick.

Up on the house - top click, click, click, Down thro' the chim - ney... with good Saint Nick.

Sleigh Ride

[PARISH AND ANDERSON]

Just hear those sleigh bells jingling,
    ring-ting-tingling, too,
Come on, it's lovely weather for a sleigh
    ride together with you,
Outside the snow is falling and friends
    are calling "Yoo hoo,"
Come on, it's lovely weather for a sleigh
    ride together with you.

Giddy-yap, giddy-yap, giddy-yap, let's go,
Let's look at the show,
We're riding in a wonderland of snow.
Giddy-yap, giddy-yap, giddy-yap, it's grand,
Just holding your hand.
We're gliding along with a song
Of a wintery fairy-land.

Our cheeks are nice and rosy, and comfy
    cozy are we,
We're snuggled up together like two birds
    of a feather would be.
Let's take that road before us and sing a
    chorus or two
Come on, it's lovely weather for a sleigh
    ride together with you.

Moderately bright

Just hear those sleigh bells jin-gle-ing, ring-ting-tin-gle-ing, too,——

— come on it's love-ly weather for a sleigh ride to-geth-er with you.

Feliz Navidad

[FELICIANO]

Feliz Navidad. Feliz Navidad. Feliz Navidad.
Prospero año y felicidad. Feliz Navidad.

I want to wish you a Merry Christmas,
With lots of presents to make you happy.
I want to wish you a Merry Christmas
From the bottom of my heart.

I want to wish you a Merry Christmas
With mistletoe and lots of cheer,
With lots of laughter throughout the years
From the bottom of my heart.

Jingle Bell Rock

[BEAL AND BOOTHE]

Jingle bell, jingle bell, jingle bell rock
Jingle bell swing and jingle bells ring
Snowin' and blowin' up bushels of fun
Now the jingle hop has begun.

Jingle bell, jingle bell, jingle bell rock
Jingle bells chime in jingle bell time.
Dancin' and prancin' in jingle bell square
In the frosty air.

What a bright time, it's the right time
To rock the night away.
Jingle bell time, is a swell time
To go glidin' in a one-horse sleigh.

Giddy-up jingle-horse pick up your feet
Jingle around the clock;
Mix and mingle in a jinglin' beat
That's the Jingle Bell Rock.

That's the Jingle Bell Rock.

The Little Drummer Boy

[Davis, Onorati, and Simeone]

Come they told me pa rum pum
pum pum,
A new born King to see, pa rum pum
pum pum,
Our finest gifts we bring pa rum pum
pum pum
To lay before the King pa rum pum
pum pum rum pum pum pum,
rum pum pum pum
So to honor Him pa rum pum pum pum
When we come.

Little Baby pa rum pum pum pum
I am a poor boy too, pa rum pum
pum pum
I have no gift to bring pa rum pum
pum pum
That's fit to give our King pa rum pum
pum pum rum pum pum pum,
rum pum pum pum
Shall I play for you? pa rum pum
pum pum
On my drum.

Mary nodded pa rum pum pum pum
The Ox and Lamb kept time pa rum
pum pum pum
I played my drum for Him pa rum
pum pum pum
I played my best for Him pa rum pum
pum pum rum pum pum pum,
rum pum pum pum
Then He smiled at me pa rum
pum pum pum
Me and my drum.

Come they told me pa rum pum pum pum,

A new born King to see pa rum pum pum pum

Silver Bells

[LIVINGSTON AND EVANS]

City sidewalks, busy sidewalks
Dressed in holiday style.
In the air there's a feeling of Christmas.
Children laughing, people passing
Meeting smile after smile,
And on ev'ry street corner you hear:

Silver bells, silver bells,
It's Christmas time in the city.
Ring-a-ling, hear them ring,
Soon it will be Christmas day.

City streetlights, even stop lights
Blink a bright red and green,
As the shoppers rush home with their treasures.
Hear the snow crunch, see the kids bunch,
This is Santa's big scene,
And above all this bustle you hear:

Silver bells, silver bells,
It's Christmas time in the city.
Ring-a-ling hear them ring,
Soon it will be Christmas day.

Sil-ver bells, — (sil-ver bells) sil-ver bells, — (sil-ver bells)

It's Christ-mas time in the cit - y.

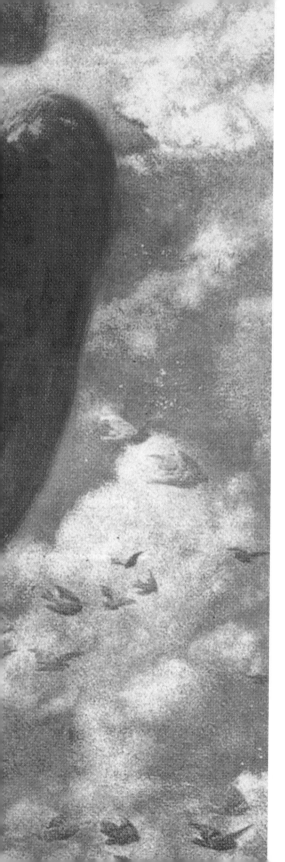

Silent Night

[MOHR AND GRUBER]

Silent night, holy night,
All is calm, all is bright.
Round yon Virgin Mother and Child
Holy Infant so tender and mild,
Sleep in heavenly peace,
Sleep in heavenly peace.

Silent night, holy night,
Shepherds quake at the sight.
Glories stream from heaven afar,
Heavenly hosts sing Alleluia,
Christ the Savior is born,
Christ the Savior is born.

Silent night, holy night,
Son of God love's pure light.
Radiant beams from Thy holy face,
With the dawn of redeeming grace,
Jesus Lord at Thy birth.
Jesus Lord at Thy birth.

Quietly

Si - lent night, ho - ly night,

All is calm, all is bright.

Christmas Is Coming

[TRADITIONAL WELSH CAROL]

Christmas is coming,
The goose is getting fat.
Please put a penny
In the old man's hat.
If you haven't a penny,
A half-penny will do.
If you haven't a half-penny
God bless you!

Christmas is coming,
God bless you!
Christmas is coming,
May your wishes all come true!

Christ-mas is com-ing, God bless you! Christ-mas is com-ing, May your wish-es all come true!

Have Yourself a Merry Little Christmas

[MARTIN AND BLANE]

Have yourself a merry little Christmas,
Let your heart be light,
From now on our troubles
Will be out of sight.

Have yourself a merry little Christmas,
Make the yuletide gay,
From now on our troubles
Will be miles away.

Here we are as in olden days,
Happy golden days of yore,
Faithful friends who are dear to us
Gather near to us once more.

Through the years we all will be together
If the fates allow,
Hang a shining star up on the highest bough
And have yourself a merry little Christmas now.

Moderately

Have your-self a   mer-ry lit-tle Christ-mas, let your heart be   light,   From now on our trou-bles Will be out of sight.

O Children Wake

[DIAMOND]

The hedgerows glitter,
The dark woods shine
In dresses of sparkling white.
For while we slumbered,
The Ice Queen passed
All over the earth last night.

O Children, wake,
For a fairy world
Is waiting for you and me,
With gems aglow
On the moonlit grass,
And jewels on every tree.

O Children, wake!
To a jewel day.
O Children, wake!
To a jewel day.

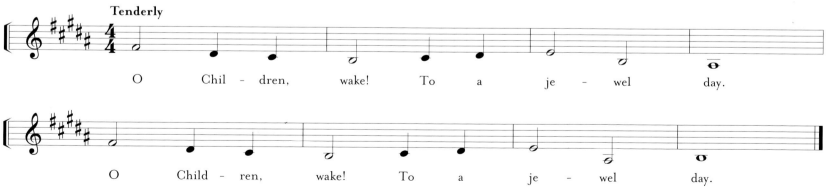

I Saw Mommy Kissing Santa Claus

[CONNOR]

I saw Mommy kissing Santa Claus,
Underneath the mistletoe last night;
She didn't see me creep
down the stairs to have a peep,
She thought that I was tucked
Up in my bedroom fast asleep.

Then I saw Mommy tickle Santa Claus,
Underneath his beard so snowy white;
Oh what a laugh it would have been,
If Daddy had only seen
Mommy kissing Santa Claus last night.

Moderately slow

I saw Mom-my kiss-ing San - ta Claus, Un-der-neath the mis-tle-toe last night;

Auld Lang Syne

[BURNS]

Should auld acquaintance be forgot,
And never brought to mind?
Should auld acquaintance be forgot,
And days of Auld Lang Syne?

For Auld Lang Syne, my dear
For Auld Lang Syne,
We'll take a cup of kindness yet,
For Auld Lang Syne.

Should auld ac-quaint-ance be for-got, And—

nev-er brought to mind? Should auld ac-quaint-ance

be for-got, And— days of Auld Lang Syne?

Ave Maria

[Scott, Gounod, and Schubert]

Ave Maria!
Oh listen to our little prayer.
We pray, Oh Maria,
 maiden mild,
For Thou can save us
 from yonder wild.
And Thou can save us
 from despair.
Save us from despair!
May we sleep safely
 in Thy care,
In Thy care.

Ave Maria!
Oh we raise our voices.
In the great goodness,
Each heart rejoices.
Lord 'tis Thy greatness
Fills earth and heaven,
Honor and praises
To Thee be given.
Ave Maria!
Oh Ave Maria.

Slowly

We pray,—Oh Ma - ri - a, maid-en

mild,—————————— For Thou— can

save us from yon - der wild.

Away in a Manger

[MURRAY]

Away in a manger no crib for a bed,
The little Lord Jesus laid down His sweet head.
The stars in the sky looked down where He lay,
The little Lord Jesus asleep on the hay.

The cattle are lowing, the Baby awakes,
But little Lord Jesus no crying He makes.
I love Thee, Lord Jesus, look down from the sky,
And stay by my cradle till morning is nigh.

Be near me, Lord Jesus, I ask Thee to stay,
Close by me forever and love me, I pray;
Bless all the dear children in Thy tender care,
And take us to heaven, to live with Thee there.

A - way in a man-ger no crib for a bed, The lit - tle Lord Je - sus laid down His sweet head.

Jingle Bells

[PIERPONT]

Dashing through the snow
In a one horse open sleigh,
O'er the fields we go,
Laughing all the way.

Bells on bobtail ring,
Making spirits bright,
What fun it is to ride and sing
A sleighing song tonight.

Oh! Jingle bells! Jingle bells!
Jingle all the way!
Oh, what fun it is to ride
In a one horse open sleigh,
Hey! Jingle bells! Jingle bells!
Jingle all the way!
Oh, what fun it is to ride
In a one horse open sleigh!

Oh! Jin-gle bells! Jin-gle bells! Jin-gle all the way! Oh, what fun it is to ride in a one horse o-pen sleigh,

Hey! Jin-gle bells! Jin-gle bells! Jin-gle all the way! Oh, what fun it is to ride in a one horse o-pen sleigh!

The First Noël

[TRADITIONAL ENGLISH CAROL]

The first Noël, the angel did say,
Was to certain poor shepherds in fields as they lay;
In fields where they lay keeping their sheep,
On a cold winter's night that was so deep.

Noël, Noël, Noël, Noël,
Born is the King of Israel.

No - ël,— No - ël, No - ël, No-

ël, Born is the King - of Is - ra - el.

O Little Town of Bethlehem

[BROOKS AND REDNER]

O little town of Bethlehem,
How still we see thee lie!
Above thy deep and dreamless sleep
The silent stars go by;
Yet in thy dark streets shineth
The everlasting light;
The hopes and fears of all the years
Are met in thee tonight.

For Christ is born of Mary
And gathered all above,
While mortals sleep, the angels keep
Their watch of wond'ring love.
O morning stars, together
Proclaim the holy birth!
And praised sing to God the King,
And peace to men on Earth!

God Rest Ye Merry, Gentlemen

[ENGLISH TRADITIONAL]

God rest ye merry, gentlemen
Let nothing you dismay,
Remember, Christ our Savior
Was born on Christmas Day,
To save us all from Satan's pow'r
When we were gone astry.

O tidings of comfort and joy,
Comfort and joy;
O tidings of comfort and joy!

Moderately

O— ti-dings of com - fort and joy, Com-fort and joy; O— tid - ings of com - fort and joy!

The Little Saint Nick

[WILSON]

Well, a way up north
Where the air is cold,
There's a tale about Christmas
That you've all been told,
And a real famous cat
All dressed in red,
How he spends the whole year,
workin' out of his sled.
It's the Little Saint Nick,
It's the Little Saint Nick

And haulin' through the snow
At a frightening speed,
With a half a dozen deer
With old Rudy in the lead,
He oughta wear goggles
Cause the snow really flies,
And he's leaving every pad
With a little surprise.
It's the Little Saint Nick
It's the Little Saint Nick

Run, run reindeer
Run, run reindeer

Run, run rein - deer——

Run, run rein - deer——

Frosty the Snowman

[Nelson and Rollins]

Frosty the Snowman was a jolly happy soul
With a corncob pipe and a button nose
and two eyes made out of coal.
Frosty the Snowman is a fairy tale they say;
He was made of snow but the children
know how he came to life one day.

There must have been some magic in that
old silk hat they found;
For when they placed it on his head he
began to dance around.
Oh Frosty the Snowman was alive as he
could be;
And the children say he could laugh and
play just the same as you and me.

Frosty the Snowman knew the sun was
hot that day;
So he said, "Let's run and we'll have
some fun now before I melt away."
Down to the village with a broomstick
in his hand,
Running here and there all around the
square sayin' "catch me if you can."

He led them down the streets of town
right to the traffic cop;
And he only paused a moment when he
heard him holler "stop!"
For Frosty the Snowman had to hurry on
his way;
But he waved goodbye sayin', "Don't you
cry. I'll be back again someday."

Thumpety thump thump, Thumpety
thump thump, look at Frosty go.
Thumpety thump thump, Thumpety
thump thump, over the hills of snow.

Brightly

Fros — ty the Snow-man was a jol-ly hap-py soul—— With a

corn-cob pipe and a but-ton nose— and two eyes made out of coal.

If Every Day Was Like Christmas

[WEST]

I hear the bells,
Saying Christmas is here.
They ring out to tell the world
That this is the season of cheer.

Oh why can't every day be like Christmas?
Why can't that feeling go on endlessly?
For if every day could be just like Christmas
What a wonderful world this would be.

For if ev - ery day—— could be

just like Christ-mas, what a won-der-ful

world—— this would be——

Happy Xmas

[Ono and Lennon]

So this is Christmas
And what have you done?
Another year over
And a new one just begun;

And so this is Christmas,
I hope you have fun
The near and the dear ones
The old and the young.

A merry merry Christmas
And a happy New Year
Let's hope it's a good one
Without any fear.

And so this is Christmas
For weak and for strong
For the rich and the poor ones
The road is so long.

A merry merry Christmas
And a happy New Year
Let's hope it's a good one
Without any fear.

And so this is Christmas
For black and for white
For the yellow and red ones
Let's stop all the fights.

A very merry Christmas
And a happy New Year
Let's hope it's a good one
Without any fear.

A ve-ry mer-ry Christ-mas—— And a hap-py New Year Let's hope it's a good one—— With-out a-ny fear.

Joy to the World

[WATTS AND MASON]

Joy to the world!
The Lord is come:
Let earth receive her King.
Let ev'ry heart prepare Him room,
And heav'n and nature sing,
And heav'n and nature sing,
And heaven and heaven and nature sing.

Joy to the world!
The Savior reigns:
Let men their songs employ,
While fields and floods, rocks, hills
  and plains,
Repeat the sounding joy,
Repeat the sounding joy,
Repeat, repeat the sounding joy.

He rules the world
with truth and grace,
And makes the nations prove
The glories of his righteousness,
And wonders of his love,
And wonders of his love,
And wonders, wonders of his love.

MUSIC

We wish to thank the following properties whose cooperation has made this unique collection possible. All care has been taken to trace ownership of these selections and to make a full acknowledgment. If any errors or omissions have occurred, they will be corrected in subsequent editions, provided notification is sent to the authors.

"All I Want for Christmas Is My Two Front Teeth" © 1946 by Warner Brothers, Inc.

"The Christmas Song" © 1946, 1974 by Edwin H. Morris & Co., A Division of MPL Inc.

"Feliz Navidad" © 1970 by J&H Pub., Co.

"Frosty the Snowman" © 1950 by Chappell & Co.

"Happy Xmas" © 1971 by Lenono Music.

"Have Yourself a Merry Little Christmas" © 1943 by EMI-Feist Catalog.

"Here Comes Santa Claus" © 1947, 1970 by Warner Brothers, Inc.

"I Saw Mommy Kissing Santa Claus" © 1952 Regent Music Corp.; © 1980 Jewel Music Pub. Co., Inc.

"If Every Day Was Like Christmas" © 1965 by Atlantic Music Corp.

"I'll Be Home for Christmas" © 1948, 1956 by Gannon and Kent Music Co.

"It's Beginning To Look Like Christmas" © 1951 by Frank Music Corp.

"It's the Most Wonderful Time of the Year" © 1963 by Barnaby Music Corp./Criterian Music.

"Jingle Bell Rock" © 1957 by Chappell & Co.

"Let It Snow! Let It Snow! Let It Snow!" © 1945 by Cahn Music Co.

"The Little Drummer Boy" © 1958, 1960 by Mills Music, Inc.

"The Little Saint Nick" © 1963 by Irving Music Inc.

"Rockin' Around the Christmas Tree" © 1958, 1986 by St. Nicholas Music Inc.

"Rudolph, the Red-nosed Reindeer" © 1949, 1977 by St. Nicholas Music Inc.

"Santa Claus Is Coming to Town" © 1934, 1962 by Leo Feist, Inc.

"Silver Bells" © 1950, 1977 by Paramount Music Corporation.

"Sleigh Ride" © 1948, 1950 by Mills Music, Inc.

"Winter Wonderland" © 1934 by Warner Bros. Inc.

ILLUSTRATIONS